D0341057

THE LIFEBOAT THAT SAVED THE WORLD

IRVING FINKEL

THE LIFEBOAT THAT SAVED THE WORLD

ILLUSTRATED BY DYLAN GILES

Thames & Hudson

First published in 2017 in the United States of America by Thames & Hudson Inc., 500 Fifth Avenue, New York, New York 10110

www.thamesandhudsonusa.com

Library of Congress Control Number
2017934850

ISBN 978-0-500-65122-3

Manufactured in China by Imago

CONTENTS

Background to the Story

Four thousand years ago, long before the Old
Testament came to be written down, the Sumerians
and Babylonians of ancient Mesopotamia knew the
story of the flood and the special boat that would
rescue the animals. Mesopotamia, land of the rivers
Euphrates and Tigris, is the country that today is
called Iraq. The ancient Babylonian hero — just like
Noah and his Ark in the Hebrew Bible later on — was
ordered to build a lifeboat in which animals in pairs
would be safe until the great flood was over, ready for
the new world. This man's name was Atra-hasis, the
Babylonian for "very wise," and it is the story of this
man and his remarkable boat that is recounted in
this book.

How is it possible that we can know such an ancient
story after four thousand years? The answer is that,
luckily for us, stories like this were written down
all that time ago by hard-working Mesopotamian
storytellers and scribes. These long-dead writers had
neither pencil nor paper but their writing, called

*cuneiform, was impressed with a chopstick-like
implement on tablets made from riverbank clay.
Cuneiform signs spelled out the syllables that made
up each word. An ancient Babylonian who heard our
word "apple" would use the sign pronounced "ap-"
followed by the sign pronounced "-pul" and end up
with "appul," which we could understand even if that
spelling looks funny.*

*Quite unexpectedly their clay tablets, buried in the
ground, have often managed to survive, waiting for
archaeologists to dig them up thousands of years
later so we can read their messages. When people
see a cuneiform inscription on a tablet for the first
time they usually can hardly believe that it can be
real writing — which it certainly is — or that we can
understand it today — which we certainly can!
Cuneiform existed long before the alphabet was
invented, and is the oldest type of writing that we
know of. By 200 AD cuneiform writing had become
as extinct as any dinosaur, and it was not until about
1850 AD (when Queen Victoria was on the throne)
that brilliant scholars managed to decipher this long-
dead, wonderful writing and bring these oldest stories
back to life.*

The Babylonian story of Atra-hasis or Very-wise survives today on a handful of precious cuneiform tablets that are now looked after in different museums and archaeological collections round the world. One tablet, recently translated for the first time, explains that Atra-hasis's boat was round, the kind of riverboat that we call a coracle, and it is this discovery that has given rise to the story in this book. Atra-hasis's coracle had to be really huge — about half the size of a football field — but that is not surprising given the important job it had to do.

Atra-hasis had three sons, whose names we do not know. In this dramatic adventure the youngest son has an important part to play. We have called him Very-quick.

Where the text is written in **bold**, the words have been translated directly from the original cuneiform tablets.

Other tablets tell us about the Mesopotamian gods, and the daily life of these ancient people all that time ago.

You will see, therefore, that this story is not my invention. My job has just been to retell it.

CHAPTER 1
The Awful News

The boy Very-quick awoke in shock in the hot, liquid darkness.

He was alert at once, arms and legs rigid, ears straining at their hardest. Some disturbing sound just seconds before, unfamiliar and unidentifiable, had forced him awake. The boy lay waiting without breathing.

Then, beyond the space where his parents slept, he made out his father's voice, low and steady, apparently asking a question. His father, Atra-hasis, was not talking to his mother, though. To whom, then? Everyone was asleep; the only life was in the wind and the occasional murmurs of the livestock. Very-quick's dog lay oblivious on the floor, deep in a dream. There was something strange about the familiar voice; it did not have its usual cadence, or liveliness. His father was... *frightened.*

There was a lengthy pause, and then, far away
as if on the very edge of the wind, the boy seemed
to hear a whispered summons rushing through
the reed banks, "**Wall… wall!**" And, like an echo,
more words followed, "**Reed wall… reed wall!**"

Very-quick rose swiftly from his bedding and
slipped silently across the familiar room to the
doorway. His father stood motionless outside in
the courtyard, his back shrouded in darkness, but
everywhere before him was a quivering cold light
that the boy could not look at directly. Nor, he saw,
could his father.

There was another long pause.

Then came the Voice proper. And what a voice
it was; echoing and sonorous, each word wide and
tall and deep. He knew at once: it was a god who
was speaking.

His father stood like a statue while the Voice
swept over him.

"**Atra-hasis, pay heed to my advice that you
may live for ever! Destroy your house, build
a boat! Spurn possessions and save life!**"

The boy swallowed. Strange instructions indeed
for his father, delivered personally in the middle of

the night by a god who knew his name and where to find him. And this was not some small, quiet god who never said anything. It must be one of the Top Three whom everyone knew, God Anu, God Enlil or God Enki.

> *There were lots of gods and goddesses in ancient Mesopotamia. Anu, Enlil and Enki were, in that order, the most important three. Each god had his wife and children and usually a special area of responsibility, like agriculture or warfare. Between them they looked after everything. Most of the time they did a good job, but some could be inattentive and one or two were naughty. They each had a special crown.*

Very-quick could see that this message made no sense to his father, who remained silent, his head bowed. *Why was it necessary to close everything down and build a boat? What was the point?* Atra-hasis twisted his hands in uncertainty, then opened them wide as if in appeal.

The boy himself, however, understood immediately. A life-saving *boat* could only mean life-threatening *water*. There was going to be a flood then, a really bad flood, where nothing would be safe. And it was his own father who was going to have to build the lifeboat.

Atra-hasis, unaware of his son's presence, was breathing deeply, thinking carefully. This, the god who had come to him, could only be God Enki, for whom he had always had a soft spot...

Enki was quite different from his fellow gods, with his sense of humor and fondness for playing tricks. There were lots of stories about him, getting drunk, pursuing goddesses and getting away with all sorts of skulduggery. It was Enki in some mad mood who had once imposed all the different languages on the world, which is why there was always such laughter and hand-waving when they tried to deal with foreign traders and merchants.

Whatever all this business was now, however, it sounded serious.

"I know nothing about boats," Atra-hasis said at length.

It came out sounding defiant, defeatist even. Everybody who lived in the marshes or by the River

Tigris or the River Euphrates knew about boats. They
were just everywhere; you saw them all the time.
There were several different shapes. And river boats
weren't so complicated: a few bundles of reeds, a load
of waterproofing and there you were. If it came to say,
a real emergency; anyone could run up something
that would *float*. On the other hand, if people's lives
were going to depend on it…

Enki waited.

Atra-hasis felt he could quite reasonably ask for
a bit more information. There wasn't much to go on.
He was beginning to wonder, too, about tools and
materials.

"Draw out the boat that you will make,"
said Enki then, as if reading his thoughts, **"on a
circular plan."**

"Aha!" thought Atra-hasis, "a *round* boat. Not
so complicated, then. One of those *coracles*."

"Let her length and breadth be equal,"
continued the Voice.

Atra-hasis looked up. That made no sense at all.
Round was round. How could a circle —

"Do I have to draw it for you?"

The question, although perfectly polite, sounded a trifle sarcastic. Atra-hasis remembered the school room. Drawing a square frame round a circle on a lump of clay, trying to think of the name for the funny corner spaces and measure them. A great waste of time, he had thought it. But now it came back to him, how a circle could be said to have length and breadth. God Enki was just making sure.

Atra-hasis nodded his head. A round coracle boat. That made sense. Coracles floated marvelously; he had never heard of one sinking. And he was to build it, and life itself would be saved. Fine. Not exactly a normal day's work, but orders from Enki were orders...

Mind you, he told himself, this thing was going to have to be a lot bigger than any conventional coracle. A normal one could carry a couple of people and a goat comfortably enough, but not much more. For such a grand purpose —

"Her floor-area will have to be one whole field, and her sides twenty-three feet high," said Enki firmly.

A field? *A whole field*? His mind reeled. Atra-hasis tried to visualize it, laid out on the ground. It would take a double-hour to walk round it. It was impossible.

It would never float, it would break in half, no one could possibly find enough stuff to make it, it was utterly mad —

"You've seen rope and the rushes for boat-making many times, remember. And someone else can twist the ropes together for you," continued Enki, unperturbedly.

"I can help," thought the boy. *"We all will."*

"You will need exactly 327 miles of rope," Enki added after a delay, as if he had just worked it out in his head.

327 kilometres? Atra-hasis couldn't believe it.

A rope that long would stretch to the moon. It will take all the coracle builders in the kingdom...

And saving the whole of life. Why *me*? he wanted to ask.

But the light was fading.

God Enki had departed.

What was Atra-hasis to do about it? He couldn't possibly tell anyone, least of all his wife and the boys. If this was really going to happen he would protect them for as long as possible, he decided. He must carry this alone.

No one else could know.

Very-quick withdrew silently into the darkness
of the room and regained his bedding with a thudding
heart. There was too much to hold in his mind.
Maybe his father would be angry to discover that
he had been watching and listening. He could hear
his mother's peaceful breathing. What on earth
was going to happen?

The boy rolled over and closed his eyes. When
the time came, he would help wherever he could
with his father's giant boat, if that was what had
to be done. He liked building things.

Atra-hasis, meanwhile, remained outside in the
night air. If life had to be saved, he was thinking,
what about the *animals*? They would have to be part
of it. All living things! Four-footed, winged, wriggly;
the whole lot would have to be saved. No wonder the
boat had to be so huge.

In his mind he glimpsed for a moment what
might lie ahead and he literally staggered. It was
all unthinkable.

There was only one way forward: plunge
straightaway into work and build this lifeboat,
just as God Enki ordered.

CHAPTER 2

The Gods Make a Decision

You may well be wondering about all this. One man, who lived thousands of years ago in ancient Mesopotamia, is suddenly given the job of building the world's largest lifeboat to save all living things from death by water. How could such a state of affairs have come about?

Today, when many other stories in between have been forgotten forever, we know. At least, we know a little. The whole story was recorded by the storytellers, long afterwards, in cuneiform writing, on smooth tablets of special clay.

The gods of Babylonia, looking down on the world, were presented with a terrible plan. It was only God Enki who stepped in at the last minute...

"NO! NO! NO!"

The angry words boomed out, echoing to and fro across the upper heavens like an explosion of ferocious thunder. It was no outbreak of bad weather, however; there was no lightning to be seen, or downpour of slanting rain. It was God Enlil, in a white-hot fury, and not for the first time. He stood there as if made of stone, giant of stature, hands on hips, his head thrown back. He was a roaring, raging lion. Several of the nearby gods moved discreetly away out of sight. Up until that moment it had been a normal, peaceful afternoon, with lyre music being played somewhere, and the air sweet and fragrant. But no longer.

Enlil sometimes forgot that Anu was really the boss and he was technically only Number Two. He was moody and intolerant, and the younger gods especially knew that his temper, at its worst, was something to avoid.

"Not AGAIN! I had just dropped off! This is *it*. I have had ENOUGH! I will not put up with their confounded racket a moment longer!"

Old Anu sighed. The same old story with Enlil, he thought. Moan, moan, moan. Mind you, it was true, there was a dreadful hubbub again from below; and it *was* a bit much sometimes. And Enlil was right in one thing: it was certainly worse than it used to be. He peered carefully down through the clouds, trying to understand why the living world had become so noisy.

Far beneath lay the land between the great rivers; he could make out the familiar mountains and the marshlands, the cities and towns, the villages and farms. People everywhere were struggling and pushing for food and water or space and air; others fought for property and riches or power and control. There was an insistent clamor of argument overlaid with conflict, and, on top of that, borne up on the wind, the endless cries of new-born babies and the groans of the dying. In the background, animals large and small, tame and wild weren't much better; often the rising sweetness of birdsong that all the gods loved could hardly make itself heard. It was the same situation everywhere he looked.

This noise problem had come up before, once or twice with dire consequences. The first time Enlil had sent a punishing plague, and after that a deadly drought. On each occasion the sufferings of the people had been unbearable before mercy had been shown, and no one liked to think about that any more. Recently, however, there had been mutterings by other gods about the noise problem. Now, for the umpteenth time, Enlil had been jerked awake while dozing off after a good meal, sprawled in his special chair. This looked like the final straw. In fact, thought Anu, the situation was decidedly ominous.

Behind him now Enlil was stomping heavily up and down, frowning and scowling. Smoke seemed to be coming out of him as his eyes flashed and his great fists opened and shut. But then, in a way that was even more disturbing, he grew completely calm. He had obviously come to some decision. Enlil clapped his hands together for attention (not that any of the gods within earshot had been ignoring him) for, as was his right, he was summoning them there and then to a high-level meeting.

The gods looked at one another in consternation. No one had forgotten the earlier disasters that had been imposed on the world beneath, and no one wanted change of any kind, but with Enlil in this sort of mood nothing was safe. Everyone had to be there. They could all choose whether to speak or to vote, but attendance was obligatory.

When they had all finally taken their seats in the debating chamber, Enlil made it clear right away who was in control. The gods listened in complete silence.

He had a particularly grim proposal for settling the problem of noise, and, since he was no longer shouting in anger, everyone could see that this latest idea had been in his mind for some time.

"This whole creation business has been mishandled from day one," he declared. "There are far too many human beings down there, and they don't work hard enough, and their primitive, noisy lifestyle shatters the austere calm needed by us gods. What is more, they all live too long."

He gesticulated with both hands, holding their attention.

"We up here are in charge of everything, are we not? We organize everything, work out whatever is going to happen, and make it all fit together. Who of us gets uninterrupted, much-deserved sleep? Enough is enough. It's over, I'm telling you."

There was an unclear rumble in response. None of the other gods felt as strongly about it and many thought Enlil's reaction was over the top. Some of the older gods, truth to tell, didn't hear so well anyway and could fall asleep without trouble whatever was happening around them. But Enlil raised his hand imperiously.

"I repeat, it is over. I have reached this point before, you will remember; I have tried disease, I have tried starvation, but now I condemn the whole lot to *death by water*, once and for all. I am commissioning an overwhelming *deluge* such as has never been seen before and there's an end of it."

There was a gasp of horror round the walls of the chamber. The gods looked wordlessly at one another. *Annihilating* the noisemakers was the last thing

anyone would have suggested. It was murderous madness, no kind of solution at all. If things were really that bad...

"Couldn't we just try asking them to be a bit quieter?" asked a village god who didn't usually speak up.

"We could, you know," came another voice. "Firmly but politely. We never have actually *asked* them, have we?"

Enlil snorted.

"There are new ones born every minute. It is chock-a-block down there! There is no end to the little nuisances with their screeching and scrabbling."

"I have better idea," said Goddess Ishtar. (Love and War were her specialities, and she was heartbroken to think of her loyal devotees suffering such a fate.) "Couldn't we all relocate to a higher level? It goes up and up, doesn't it?" —

she pointed upwards.

"We could just move all this"— she gestured with her hands — "upstairs. Out of earshot. It would take no time at all if everyone helped."

Many gods seated around the chamber nodded in agreement or made supportive noises.

"Nonsense. That is preposterous, Ishtar. Out of the question. This human-being thing is out of date and they are not what we need. We start again from the beginning. I have spoken."

One or two tried to catch the eye of God Adad, who was responsible for the weather and had all the storms in the world under his control. If *he* refused to cooperate …

Adad looked at the floor. He was trying to make himself inconspicuous, hoping the matter would blow over without his participation.

Anu was no better. He was a more reflective god than Enlil, and remembered things that had happened before many of his fellow gods were even born, and that meant he was always present in the background to steady things. Today, though, he seemed withdrawn and they could see that he was not going to come up with any kind of counter-argument.

Enlil surveyed the discussion chamber with a magisterial eye. So far the matter had been going his way, but he looked pointedly over at Number Three, God Enki, who was famously unpredictable and a dangerously effective speaker. If trouble was going to come from any quarter, that would be it.

There was a lot of conversation now, voices rising and falling in indignation and disbelief. Enlil stood unmoved at the podium. People were looking to Enki to speak.

Enki was always popular and could be confident that his views would be listened to, but he knew better than to take on Enlil in front of everybody when feelings were running so

high. In his view, of course, killing off all living things
would be horrendous: the plan — like the earlier
attempts — was cruel, wasteful and wrong. He himself
was genuinely fond of the humans and animals
who disported themselves below, day after day; the
spectacle was always changing and never boring, and
actually, he liked to be helpful wherever possible.
There was no point in saying all that, though. He
stood and waited for silence.

"There is, you know, an angle that our Chairman
seems to have overlooked completely. Who but for
poor old mankind is going to minister to us gods,
feeding us and caring for our statues in the temples,
singing our praises and generally making us all
feel good?"

There was a noticeable lightening in the assembly.
What a good point! Good old Enki...

The question as to who would do the gods'
cooking had, however, already occurred to Enlil.
"Not at all. My scheme is that — once they have
all been annihilated — I will propose that Mother
Goddess" — here he bowed respectfully in her
direction, — "should be invited to create a more
suitable replacement: harder working creatures, for

one thing, and silent too. I was thinking it might be
a good idea if these new-type servants would only be
allowed to communicate by waving their hands."

The Mother Goddess lowered her eyes. She loved
her creations, every single one, and she was too
appalled to speak.

"So," Enlil continued aloud, choosing his moment,
summing up, "this is what is going to happen.
Universal death by drowning."

He looked across for support at God Adad, who
was shaking his head in disbelief.

"See to it, please. I shall issue full instructions.
And the whole thing is to be kept secret outside
the walls of this chamber. Not a word."

Gods moved off into small groups, discussing
what they had just heard in an undertone. Many
were white-faced and trembling; others clung to one
another, weeping. Enlil was unimpressed: there would
be no real resistance when it came to it. He turned
his back on them all, beckoned peremptorily to Adad
and they walked off together, Enlil still talking.

God Enki, meanwhile, remained in his seat,
staring into space and thinking hard. He was certainly
going to intervene, not with persuasive speechifying

or brilliant public arguments, but by operating on the quiet, behind the scenes. If he couldn't prevent wholesale destruction on his own he could certainly ensure that a handpicked collection of humans and animals would survive, somehow or other; life in all its variety would carry on again after Enlil's insane disaster.

How to achieve that? he wondered.

Well, Enlil's latest method for extinguishing life was going to be a universal flood. There was only one possible solution for that sort of nonsense, wasn't there? Someone down there would have to build a boat...

CHAPTER 3
To Build a Boat

"You heard about this giant boat business?"

"Sounds completely loopy to me."

"Me too. Let's go and hear what he has to say."

The two men, who lived nearby, joined a group of people who had heard peculiar rumors and were now milling about by a cluster of date palms, talking them over.

Atra-hasis was on his way to meet them, taking young Very-quick with him, explaining as they walked that he needed helpers to build a superhuman boat.

"I know."

"You know? What can you know?"

"I couldn't sleep. The night before last. I was there. I... heard everything."

Atra-hasis stopped in his tracks, speechless. He had been plodding about all day yesterday, unable to settle at anything, running over Enki's words in his mind, alone with his problem. "What's wrong, Hassy?"

his wife had asked more than once, but he had been unable to tell her. And all that time Very-quick had been in the know.

"I couldn't help it. I just woke up. But I can help you. Run and do things. I can be your assistant."

No nine-year old should have to think about the end of the world and how to prevent it. This development was not at all what Atra-hasis would have chosen, but now it had happened, it was welcome. The boy was clever and perceptive, the brightest of his sons. Atra-hasis looked down at him and they stared at one another.

Atra-hasis obviously had a real bee in his bonnet, the local men told one another: he wanted a brand-new coracle built, the biggest in the world, and he wanted it fast. They liked a challenge, of course, anybody would. But there were still awkward questions.

"What's the point?" someone called out.

"Yeah, that's what I want to know. Why so gigantic? What's wrong with the usual size? And what are you going to do with it when you've built it?"

"Exactly; it is all very well asking people to help build it, but why should they?"

The loudest questioners sounded truculent.
Atra-hasis spoke quietly.

*God Enki had already told him what to say about what
had been going on in heaven if there was any trouble.
Enki — as we know — had been on bad terms with his
superior, Enlil, recently and this would naturally make
life uncomfortable for Atra-hasis, who was under Enki's
special protection. All Babylonians were under the
protection of one of the gods. When a baby was born
it was decided in the family which one it would be.
In Atra-hasis's case it was Enki. The only solution
under these circumstances was for him and his family
to leave their home and go away. Even his critics
would understand that.*

"So you see," he concluded, "I have no choice.
I must do as Enki has instructed me. And it was
Enki himself who said we would need a boat,
and he told me how big it had to be. I am just
doing what he asked me to do."
    People nodded in understanding and many left
it at that, but there were still points to be answered.
A huge job of work was involved: why should they,

with their own work to do and their own families to look after, get involved in Atra-hasis's private project?

"Fair enough. I am no boat builder, as you know. Anyone with expertise and time who could lend a hand will be well fed and looked after, and, I hope, will get something more when it is completed. I cannot promise much. But it will be an adventure and a challenge. And I dare say our great boat will become famous one day."

That was an appealing idea.

In the end a group of the local men who — like their fathers and grandfathers before them — had been building coracles together for years agreed the idea sounded interesting from a professional point of view. Atra-hasis could obviously never pull the thing off alone and the fact that God Enki had personally instructed him in what to do was very persuasive. Friends or neighbors who were woodworkers or bitumen experts started volunteering, and, before long, Atra-hasis had a team. The final appeal was for an experienced shipwright to be in charge. A good man came forward.

In addition to the huge size, Atra-hasis explained, they only had *seven days to complete the work*. The

freshly recruited workmen looked at one another
open-mouthed. Was he serious? Seven days? Yes,
it was official. Enki had said so, and recommended
that a water clock to monitor the passing of the work
hours for everybody would be helpful. His young
assistant Very-quick would be in charge of that.
Nobody else would be allowed to touch it.

Atra-hasis stretched out expressive arms and said
something vague about building his new coracle in
a field. That was odd, too; wouldn't it be more
sensible to construct it right next to the river?
He had shook his head. No need. They followed
him and his assistant in a straggle.

"What we need here," said Atra-hasis, opening
his sack, "is one of those old-fashioned peg and
string devices."

He planted the peg in the middle of the field
and pulled the string taut.

"Play us a tune, then," said somebody.

"Are you expecting that to grow into a tree?"
asked somebody else.

Atra-hasis laughed.

As Very-quick planted his foot firmly on the peg-
head his father pulled the string taut and began to

walk steadily round in a great circle, marking
the perimeter line for the walls of his round boat.
Atra-hasis concentrated, not looking up, and the
people fell quiet. His authority was unmistakeable
and all those who were watching him knew then that
the plan, however mad it sounded, was going to work.

Unknown to the boy, Enki had already spoken
to his father again. He had warned Atra-hasis that a
strange sign would come when the flood was really
imminent: birds and fish would rain down on them.
The fatal time would be the day of the new moon, for
that was when the gods "upstairs" had arranged for
the watery annihilation to begin. Atra-hasis refused to
think about that now. He had many things to do and
not much time to do them in. He braced himself for
the great task.

To the new captain's great relief his workers
turned up the next day with their tools and the first
consignment of materials: palm-tree pith for the
rope and good wood for the ribs. (He hadn't dare tell
them yet how much they were going to require by
the time they were through.) Bitumen would be easy:
there were places where the stuff just bubbled blackly
out of the ground and all boat builders or anybody

else needing to waterproof something just helped themselves.

The rope-makers got down to work straightaway. They showed Atra-hasis how to twist the stuff from the date palms into the right sort of rope, but he was not very adept at it and he saw them grin at one another, stopping him before he got blisters on his palms.

Once there was a good supply the workmen began trailing the brand new rope round the circle

that Atra-hasis had marked in the field. Half way round they stopped and looked at one another open-mouthed.

"I don't believe this!"

"Look at the size of the thing!"

But, despite their apprehensions, all they had to do was to follow their normal coracle building techniques. It was exactly the same procedure, but on a colossal scale.

"Think of yourselves as giants," said Atra-hasis, "for that is what you are."

More rope had to be laid on top of the first completed circle and the two rows lashed firmly together. Row followed upon row, so that there gradually grew up on the first day a great round enclosure, the coiled snakes of tough rope laced and bound together. The record-breaking coracle was, at the beginning, nothing more than a gigantic floppy basket.

Construction got more complicated as the walls grew higher, and eventually the men in the front line had to work on ladders, heaving great lengths of rope up together to set them on top for the next stage. Assistant Very-quick liked to squat on top, passing them tools and talking. The rope-men were glad to see him.

"Pretty weird boat, your Dad wants."

"I know. He never wanted a boat before."

"Did he actually see that Enki himself, Very-quick?"

"I think he just heard his voice, telling him what to do."

"I'da heard that, I'da died of fright."

"Me too."

"What I don't understand, kid, is why it has to be

so *big*. By the time we have finished you will be able to stack all the real coracles from the river inside it and no one would know they were there."

"Why would anyone want to do that?"

"You tell me."

"I know what it might be," said the boy, as if struck by a sudden idea.

"Well?"

"A surprise birthday present!"

"Oh, sure. You must be right. No one could possibly notice that we are up to anything."

He tugged at the rope lashing and twisted it tight with the wooden pin.

"But why build it here, away from the water?" asked the next craftsman. "That's what puzzles me."

"There is not enough space near the river," said the boy. "For all the people and all the stuff. My father worked it out. We have to do it here."

"When it's done we'll have to turn it on edge and wheel it like a hoop down to the water."

"I am not sure there will be enough water in that river to float it."

The first rope-man poked him in the ribs.

"If I am to show you how to use this twisting pin properly, you have to stop talking and start paying attention. One careless slip and..."

He held up his hand. One finger had long since lost the last joint.

The carpenters, meanwhile, with adze and plane, were cutting the ribs out of the right sort of wood. This, too, was a tricky matter, for each curved rib had to fit snugly inside the rope walls, running from the top edge right down to the bottom, where the lower end fitted in the middle with the other ribs to form a plank floor. Atra-hasis insisted that his long wooden ribs be fat and beefy, for they had a crucial task to fulfil.

He was pleased with the result. He decided to report back to God Enki, calling out in a ringing voice after the second day's work, gazing upward in the dusk: **"I set in place thirty ribs that were one barley-barrel thick, sixt-six yards long."** No one but his son was there to hear. There was no detectable response from Enki, but they both knew that the message got through.

Certain toughs followed Very-quick the next morning and jeered at him, saying that his father was

mad, and that his *mad* boat would disappear off the
edge of the world and that would be *the end of them*.
But Very-quick found he just wasn't scared of them.
Perhaps it was because he had heard the voice of Enki
himself. He wasn't scared at all. Nor was the dog,
crouched between his feet, watching them steadily.

"We're going on the most interesting voyage
in the world. Places you've never even heard of.
You stay at home here with your mothers and
fathers where it's nice and safe and there is plenty

of milk for you at bed time."

They looked at one another.

"Can we come with, then?"

"You'd all be homesick. And seasick. No way."

"Come on."

The boy shook his head and the dog coughed. He knew it was only a cough but the toughs thought it was a bark and left.

CHAPTER 4
Family Conference

God Enki, of course, was hardly on call when
it came to practical problems, and there were
plenty of those. It was the shipwright who
pointed out on the third day that such a boat,
with any sort of long voyage ahead, would need
a *roof*, even though river-coracles were traditionally
open to the sky. Water would get in, wouldn't it?
Atra-hasis simply hadn't thought about that but he
agreed at once; privately he was also worrying
about on-board quarters, and how they could
arrange separate accommodation for humans
and animals.

"I must do something about the animals," he
thought for the hundredth time. "And what am
I going to tell the others?"

He was wondering whether they couldn't
fit a deck, too. The shipwright agreed.

"If we put in a deck, set in about halfway up,
it would strengthen the whole structure. I propose

cutting sturdy wooden pillars to support the new
floor, resting on the bottom planks."

"That would work well," thought Atra-hasis:
woven reed walls could be attached to the finished
pillars to mark off spaces for the different species.
"I set up 3,600 stanchions within her," he
later reported proudly to Enki once they were
all in place, **"that are half a barley-barrel thick
and ten feet high."**

Atra-hasis could not really avoid confiding
to the shipwright that he would be taking a lot
of animals with him, hence the need for special
arrangements. The man looked at him oddly
but he said nothing; he himself offered no
explanation.

The boat's profile was turning out to be rather
beautiful, silhouetted against the fading light. She was
shapely, and, despite her size, rather elegant. There
were four days left. Now is the moment, Atra-hasis
told himself, to confide properly in his wife.

"Enki came to me," he began. "He called me by
name. Enki himself told me to build this boat that
we've been working on. We're really going to need
it. Because, well, *disaster* lies ahead."

He stopped, then lowered his voice and bent towards her, speaking as quietly as he could, looking deep into her eyes.

"You see..." he went on, "Enki came to our house..."

She took the shocking news better than he expected, sitting with Very-quick, looking wide-eyed at her husband and just holding his hand. Perhaps she had already half-guessed the truth, he thought. She often knew what was going to happen before it happened. As the meaning of his words became clear in her mind she thought of children, first her own, of course, and then all the other children she knew or had seen or who must exist somewhere in the world, all running and growing with the expectation of becoming mothers and fathers themselves, and who never, ever would.

And of the houses and temples, the solid buildings proud against the sky, and all the people who lived in them and worked for them. A single picture of the whole of mankind, spread far and wide, bright now in the sunlight and soon to be extinguished in blackness, flooded her mind in awful clarity and she swallowed several times, struggling to breathe. But the command, she now knew, was from God Enki himself, and she understood at one and the same moment that her husband, and therefore she, had no choice. Almost at once she began to focus on the first practical arrangements and necessities.

Atra-hasis sent Very-quick then to summon his older brothers. They came in together, disconcerted at the drawn face of their mother, and the deep seriousness in their father, their excited questions about the boat forgotten.

"There is... stormy weather ahead," said Atra-hasis. "I have received a warning. From —" and he pointed upwards — "and that is why I am building this great round boat. It is not for fun; it has a very serious function. I think it will turn out that we cannot be without this boat when the time comes."

"But if the rivers flood we'll be alright, won't we?" asked the oldest. "That often happens. No big emergency, is it?"

"This will be water, I imagine, such as no man has seen before."

"But why must your boat be so absolutely *gigantic*, though?" asked the other. "Everyone is talking about it. Is it so we can take everyone with us?"

"Not exactly. Your mother and I have been
told to take the animals too, just in case."

"*All* the animals?" Very-quick swallowed,
looking at his dog.

"Just enough. You two will need to tell your wives
that before too long this is going to happen; all
seven of us will be on that boat together, with lots of
animals, for a good while, until whatever is going to
take place comes to take place and finally comes to an
end. We will be safe, but not everybody else will be."

"You mean a lot of people will die?"

"As I understand it, my son, yes. Very many people.
I have appealed to the high gods but they will not
listen; it is their unwavering decision and we alone —
our family — have been singled out to do this job. You
will need to be completely brave, fearless and strong,
just as you have always been. You two must safeguard
my daughters-in-law more than ever. You and Very-
quick will have to be complete heroes."

"How long will we have to be in the boat?"

"That I do not know. But what is very important
is that *you do not tell anyone else, anyone outside our
family, what I have told you.* Do you understand, both
of you? This is an order. No one else must know.

Atra-hasis scrutinised their faces, masking his inner feeling of sympathy. They had just been informed that the world was coming to an end and their own father was in charge of saving it and that everyone else was going to die and they were going to have to take animals with them wherever they were going. And yet all around them everything was normal. It was dinnertime, with cooking smoke in the air, and all the sounds of people and livestock, near and far. It defied belief that everything would not just go on forever in the same way. Their father nodded gently.

At length they left without another word, walking close together out into the darkness.

"We all know, now," said Very-quick, "and it will not be necessary to say anything more. They will come to understand it properly in a few days. We are all so proud that it is you who have been chosen and we will not let you down."

His mother was laughing and crying at the same time and she embraced her youngest son.

"How on earth are we going to deal with all the animals? You are always so good with them," she said through her tears. "You understand them, and I think they understand you. What are we going to do?"

CHAPTER 5
Two of Every Kind

There were two particular problems about the animals that worried Atra-hasis: how to make sure they had two of *every* type, and how to pick animals that would produce lots of offspring later. You could never judge that with people; sometimes the most unlikely couples never had children, and the strongest people sometimes died all of a sudden, or after an illness that had not even seemed dangerous.

His wife nodded thoughtfully.

"Tell us exactly what Enki actually told you," she said.

"Well, actually, it was a bit confusing," said Atra-hasis. "The first thing was just the order to "save life." Later Enki mentioned something to me about clean and fat animals, whatever that meant, and then talked about birds, and domestic and wild animals."

"Probably he just meant two of each, one male and one female, applied to every single possible species," said Very-quick. "Then, when it is all over, they can all have new babies."

This was obviously what Enki must have meant because by the time the waters went down there would be no living creatures at all, and any species not represented on their boat would die out. In his confusion and worry Atra-hasis had not seen the picture so clearly before.

"We will be completely responsible for what will happen," he said. "We must rescue absolutely every kind of animal, bird, reptile and insect: the whole lot, two of each. We are going to need a list so we don't forget any."

"Good idea," said his wife. "The boys can write down all the names we can think of, and then, when the time comes, we can check that they are all there."

"I was thinking to divide them up into *domestic* animals and *wild* animals," said Atra-hasis. "When I was at tablet school they had really useful lists like that. We were supposed to learn them by heart. I wonder if I can remember them all."

"I think one of the others ought to do the writing," said Very-quick. "It always takes me ages and no one can decipher anything afterwards."

His father laughed.

"They can start first thing in the morning. It's more than just a bit of homework: you could say it's the most important list that has ever been made in the whole world and we have to get it absolutely perfect. When any of you think of any name write it down straightaway. It doesn't matter about order. I will look it over later. It must be finished by the time we go to bed tomorrow night."

"I don't think," said his mother, "that you will have to do any choosing. When the time comes, if we both think "yes" about two particular animals when they arrive, they will be the right pairs."

"Yes. Perhaps. But I am still worried about how to get them all to come to the boat in the first place and then embark safely."

"They will all turn up, Hassy; I know they will."

At first light Atra-hasis's three sons could be seen sitting in the courtyard, their heads together. Good smooth clay had been fetched up from the river and the middle son — the best writer in the family — had already made the first long tablet, ready to take dictation. He raised his writing stick expectantly, but it was not so easy to produce a list out of the air, once they started to think about it. One of them mentioned sheep. Their mother called out through the door:

"My poor boys. How can you even begin? Even our own sheep come in different shapes and sizes and have different names. And we will certainly be needing lots of wool so we will have to take fluffy ones too, not to mention a nice pair of black sheep."

"Well, we thought we'd start with two legged animals, then three, and then quadrupeds."

"*Three* legs?"

"We mustn't forget *anything*."

"OK. I'll start you off. Monkeys! Er — cows... Don't forget snakes."

Can you imagine having to make a list like that?
Thinking up the name of every species of the world's
living things? And then writing them all down —
legibly — in neat columns on your clay tablet,
not forgetting a single one, so that your own father
could call the register as his passengers lined
up to come on board the lifeboat?
It is true, though; schoolboys (and the few girls who
did go to scribal school) had to learn how to write the
names of all the animals, which would
have been helpful even if they did not know the
whole lot by heart (as they were supposed to).
Mind you, it would be even more complicated if you
had to do the same thing today. Atra-hasis's family,
four thousand years ago, could never
have known about all the animals, birds and
insects of the whole world like we do. No
Babylonian adventurer ever got to Africa or
China or Australia (although one or two might
have got to India). So, when Atra-hasis, instructed
by Enki, talked about "all" living things it meant
all that they knew about in their own corner
of the world. But that was still a plentiful and
hard-to-organize menagerie.

"I have an idea," said the oldest brother. "The farm animals are easy. We can do those last. I am more worried about the wild animals. Dad not only has to collect them up but they will have to live peacefully together on the boat, won't they? We don't want any of them eating the others. Let's divide them into *Four-Footed-Big-and-Hungry*, *Four-Footed-Medium*, *Small-and-Easily-Trampled* and, I suppose, *Practically-Invisible*. (We all know who will be in charge of those.) Then it will be easier to plan the right accommodation on board."

"Okay. Lions, tigers…"

"What about *wolves*?"

"Wolves of course. Cheetahs and leopards."

"And those horrid ones: jackals and — er — hyenas…"

"And bison. And wild boar. Anybody think of any others?"

"Lynxes. And those other large ones, what are they called? Oh yes, zebus."

"Okay that makes eleven big and hungry, two of each. Write them down."

That seemed like progress and a good way forward.

"Now for the *Mediums*. All the wild ones, like the wild sheep and wild rams; deer and stags. Aren't there more? Roe deer, gazelles, buck, foxes, wild cats, cats, caracals, mongooses, hares, tortoises and... I suppose we will have to take pigs, too."

Very-quick, meanwhile, had been running other names through his head.

"Mice, dormice, voles, shrews, jerboas, otters, martens, chameleons, jellyfish, lizards — all the different kinds, there are loads — frogs, toads, scorpions, geckos, crabs."

"Not so fast."

"And then locusts, grasshoppers, crickets, praying mantises, head lice, other lice, fleas, weevils, termites, moths, bugs, worms, earthworms, butterflies, nits, flies, horse flies, mosquitoes, gnats, wasps, water boatmen —"

"Your water boatmen are going to enjoy themselves!"

"Centipedes, spiders, dragonflies, ants, lizards —"

"You *said* lizards already!"

"Just checking."

Atra-hasis had gone off at first light to organize food supplies for the boat, musing along similar lines.

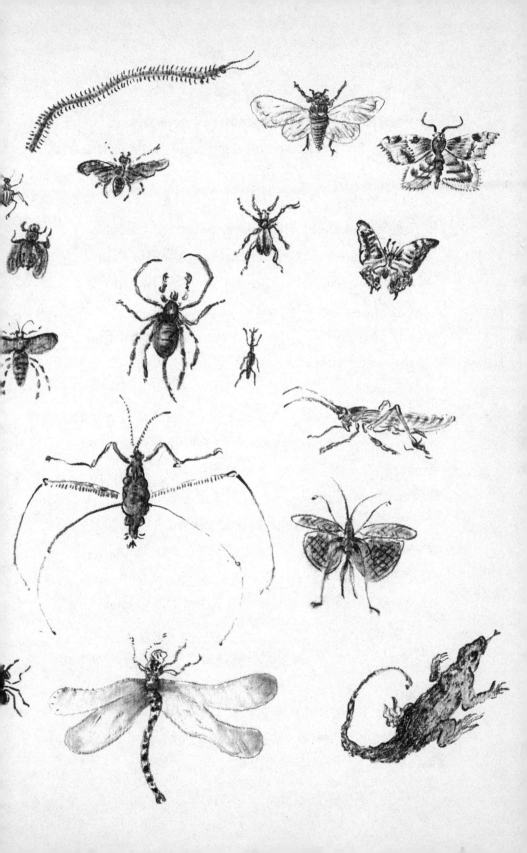

There was certainly more than one type of lion in the country, but even if he could get hold of a pair of each he couldn't take them all on board; one pair was quite enough to have to deal with. Perhaps, if they were strong and had plentiful litters when they all got off again, things would go back to how they were before. Maybe future lions descended from his two might have to go and live in cold places and grow thicker coats. The main thing was to get hold of two of each of the really different species.

"Look, Hassy," said his wife on his return, "about our list. Do we really need to take literally *everything*? I mean, what about poisonous snakes? Fleas? Bed bugs? If we, sort of, left them out, wouldn't it be better... er — later?"

Atra-hasis looked gravely at his wife. He shook his head.

"That is not for you or me to decide such things, my dear. Our job is to save every kind. And that means *every single one*."

His wife looked chastened, and Atra-hasis put his arms around her.

"Now, something important. Could you organize huge bowls of water for the different fish?" he asked.

"We'll have to catch them carefully and rush them aboard at the last minute."

"Well, we do have those large soup cauldrons. Wouldn't they do?"

"Ho ho ho! Tricked you, then, Mrs Captain! Don't you think that fish might be all right *outside* during the flood? You know, in the *water*."

"Oh, I'm not so sure, Hassy. The little fish will never cope."

"True. I suppose we will be left with the toughest ones then."

The boys, he was pleased to see, had kept hard at it, and there were two long lists (as well as squashed and rejected tablets on the floor) waiting for him by the evening. Any forgotten names could be added on a bit of extra clay. It was a comfortingly full-looking list, and clearly written, he noted with approval. He would literally be able to call the register when the time came.

"Good thing, probably," said his wife, "that there is only one type of human being."

CHAPTER 6

Poor Atra-hasis

Five full days of labor had gone by. The new, giant coracle stood waiting, fitted out exactly to Enki's specifications, and all that remained to be done was waterproofing. This turned out to be more complicated than the new captain had appreciated and he was grateful for the shipwright's expertise. Every surface, inside and out, had to be coated very carefully with bitumen, for a single leak could spell disaster. The quantities that they needed were huge, and there were different sorts and varied mixtures for those in the know. Atra-hasis was careful to report everything that had happened to Enki, with all the details:

"**I measured out one finger of bitumen for her outsides and then I measured out one finger of bitumen for her insides; I had already poured out one finger of bitumen onto her cabins. Next I caused the kilns to be loaded with three hundred and seventeen cubic yards of one kind of bitumen and I poured forty cubic yards of the other kind of bitumen within.**"

Very-quick, anxious to help, had been sent home
out of the way when the bitumen arrived. Great tubs
came down river on barges to be offloaded onto
patient donkeys, and transported one by one from
the river edge to the busy boatyard. It was a messy,
dangerous business. The bitumen had to be heated
up in great vats, bubbling up, black and stinking, the
chief worker stirring the contents like a cook bent
over some mysterious soup. The reeking mixture
had to be just right for the job, with exactly the right
consistency. That meant adding in bits of tamarisk
wood and stalks.

**"The bitumen did not
come to the surface,"**
Atra-hasis confided to
Enki, **"so I added five
fingers of lard and ordered
the kilns to be loaded
in equal measure."**

Applying the horrid
stuff was a huge job. The
thickness had to be right,
inside and out. The hot,
gooey substance had to

be spread out evenly and then smoothed over with a special wooden roller. The men worked quickly together, singing as they did so. Waterproofing with bitumen was nothing new for them, but this record-breaking job seemed to go on forever. Gradually under their hands the great boat received her black shiny coat; the liquid material hardening into a tough shell that, they promised, would keep out the water whatever the weather.

And then, just when the workmen were beginning to wonder if they could manage it, the great task was done! Atra-hasis's boat, the greatest craft ever built by man, was ready! It was a truly historic moment. Everyone involved felt proud and happy and there was a lot of rejoicing with feasting to follow.

His own family was swept up in the general excitement. The two older sons and their wives

embarked with pleasure and excitement just as soon
as they could. They rushed about examining the upper
cabins where they would be quartered, and thought
all the arrangements below utterly delightful. As he
suspected, what that boat was really going to have to
do was still beyond their comprehension. Atra-hasis
slipped away unnoticed.

It was hard to believe that Enki's superhuman
instructions could have been fulfilled to the letter
so quickly. He felt proud of his boat and his workmen;
she was a thing of beauty, poised and delicate, deep
black and gently rounded, the greatest lifeboat the
world had ever seen. From now on, however, as the
boat stood ready and their water clock began to
run down, its worried captain must look reality
in the face.

The world around him was full of the good noises
of birds and animals and adults and children, but
he could not bear it. He turned away from the very
sight of his boat. Each of the loyal workmen who
had labored on its production, their boisterous
voices ringing out behind him in the clear air, was
to perish utterly, each with his family, neighbors,
friends and enemies. All the people across the face of

their landscape; every village, every town, and even
the greatest cities that might ever be, would all, at
a contemptuous flick of God Enlil's fingers, vanish
beneath suffocating floodwater, all life snuffed out
like the pinched wick of an oil lamp.

What he just couldn't understand was this:
what had everybody done that they were all to be
so brutally punished? There were plenty of dreadful
people, to be sure; cruel and violent, cheats and
thieves, but not everybody was like that.

And when he tried to imagine the aftermath, with
himself the most responsible human being in the
whole world, he was filled with terror. Soon he must
be ruler and priest, farmer and builder, merchant and
doctor. And it would rest on his shoulders to teach
the right way forward in all things to his immediate
family, and to whatever children, grandchildren and
great-grandchildren the future would bring. He would
have to try and live to a very ripe old age if he had
to get everything up and running again for a better
world than the one before. No man before him had
ever had to face such responsibility.

But then, he reasoned to himself, the gods
would be there, watching and caring, and they would

surely be pleased when life reappeared on the earth, wouldn't they?

"Tell me," Atra-hasis cried aloud to the canopy above. "Why should the whole wonderful entity of our human world be so utterly dreadful that you, our parents, are going to write us all off as a mistake? And why should I, no better and no worse than anyone else, alone have been chosen to keep life going through their ghastly destruction?"

It was now dark. The only light was that of the great silver disc above. Using one of the building ladders, Atra-hasis climbed slowly up onto the curved roof of his waiting lifeboat. He looked out over the landscape, the great river rushing onward far away, drifting smoke and flickering lights, with the sound of peaceful evening cattle and the odd yelp of a far-distant dog.

He would call upon God Sin, the moon himself. After all, the appearance of the new moon was to be the fateful moment. Perhaps God Sin would change his ways, so that there would never be another new moon at all. Then they would all be safe.

He began to cry then, his heart overfull, weeping for all the people known to him who were doomed, and

all those people whose lives and homes could be seen from where he stood, and all those people he had never even heard of. Atra-hasis knelt with his arms outstretched, his face wet with tears, upturned to the cold, unresponsive god of the moon:

**"Let my heartbreak be extinguished!
Do you not disappear!"**

The rest of his words were drowned in sobs:

"... darkness... into my..."

But there was no comfort from the moon god, Sin; just the opposite. Sin, from his throne, swore as to the annihilation and desolation on the darkened day to come. No beseeching by him, Atra-hasis knew, would melt the heart of the resolute gods. There was nothing for it but to go ahead and load the animals. His heart sank even lower at the enormity of the task. How could he accomplish what he had to do? How could he, alone among men, bear the weight of his dreadful knowledge while the others laughed and celebrated? It was impossible.

He climbed down, distraught and sick, with wobbly legs. *"Build a boat... Save life"* had been the order; that was his job. He repeated the words to himself, over and over. What he should really be

worrying about was whether the immense and heavy
coracle would float and how to collect all the animals
and whether there would be enough room inside
for them all. He still had to organize all that. In the
moonlight he saw the slight figure of Very-quick, who
must have followed, as usual, and who now came
quietly up and stood right next to him.

"We'll be alright. You have done what you had to.
We will be together. Do not lose heart now."

Much later he stepped out into the night air, quite
alone. Dark shapes heavier than any rain or hail were
falling in profusion against the blackness of the sky
to land, twitching, at his feet. He looked down, to
find himself surrounded by the stilled bodies of fishes
and birds. Atra-hasis stooped to touch them, but they
crumbled into nothing under his fingers, and for a
moment his mind could find no explanation until
he remembered the
promised warning,
the sign that the flood
from the gods was
imminent.

CHAPTER 7

The Waters to Come

"It is happening," said Atra-hasis to his wife.
"Look, they are coming to us!"

They were standing in front of the lifeboat.
Somehow the birds, reptiles and insects came of their
own accord, arriving from every direction, two by two,
right at the feet of the captain. There was no fuss,
no squabbling and no pushing. Just two of each.
There was no need for any choosing.

So much out of the ordinary had been happening
to Atra-hasis lately that he was not even surprised
by this development. Enki must have intervened,
he thought gratefully, having a word with them all
or giving them some secret sign. Or perhaps he
despatched a messenger god to tap them on the
shoulder, one by one. At any rate, they all seemed
to have turned up. He stood by the doorway,
acknowledging each pair with a smile and nod of
welcome. Some, with short legs, took an inordinate
length of time to reach him.

They waited patiently while he checked the tablet lists and the rough plan of who should go where. Many of the smaller ones — and no doubt all the very small ones — arrived sensibly riding on the backs of the others. The two elephants were covered from head to foot with clinging passengers as they loped harmoniously and carefully together towards the waiting vessel. Eventually the last creatures were safely maneuvered through the door.

Once they were all on board Atra-hasis felt for the first time since Enki had made his shattering announcement that, perhaps, after all, he might be able to cope with what lay ahead. Provisional arrangements needed some adjustments: certain particular animals needed to be stationed further apart from one another immediately. Small, wriggly and multi-footed species were largely left to find their own quarters, with the firm warning that to chew on the fabric of the boat was forbidden under any circumstances. He had brought in huge bundles of wooden bits, rope fibers and other rough stuff piled into great baskets to provide a headquarters for them. When it came to the domestic fowls Atra-hasis brought on board more than the stipulated pair. His wife noted this with approval, obviously thinking of chicken soup, but again her husband shook his head firmly.

In the evening the shipwright turned up, as agreed, with a last bucket of pitch. Atra-hasis went out to thank his chief helper but he couldn't find the words.

"When I've gone back through the door, seal it behind me," he said at length.

"After you," said the shipwright sardonically.

"After me, the Deluge," thought Atra-hasis to himself. "Help yourself to anything you want," he added.

The shipwright grinned, and Atra-hasis could see, unable to justify himself, that the man thought he was deranged.

There was, indeed, nothing more to be said, and Atra-hasis slipped back in through the door, which the other shut tightly behind him. He could hear the swish of the bitumen roller as the shipwright, now unsupervised, did his usual, careful work round the doorframe. All the same he had taken the precaution of loading on a similar quantity in advance so that the door could be sealed all around from the inside too. Again he tried not to picture what was going to happen. The shipwright would undoubtedly move into his house and make use of whatever he could find. The beer wouldn't last long. And then, nothing but water...

He shivered and patted one of the donkeys who was nuzzling his hands as he worked, leaving a black smudge on his neck.

"Let's hope," said his middle son, noticing,
"that they won't all have to have a special mark too."

Very-quick thought of his dog. He had not been
allowed on board. They needed young and energetic
animals, his father had said firmly, two of each type.
No one was quite sure what type that dog was anyway,
and he was old and weary. The dog had looked at him
without reproach and gone outside, and was nowhere
to be found when they left the house for the last time.
Nor had his favorite frog, wriggling under his tunic,
been allowed on.

Once the door was sealed Atra-hasis, with his
wife by his side, made an announcement to all
on board, speaking slowly.

"We have all been chosen to fulfil a very special
destiny. Every living thing on this boat is IMPORTANT.
We must live peacefully and patiently on our boat,
as long as is necessary. We have arranged everything
so that everybody will have what they need during
the voyage."

He paused. His wife nodded.

"There are one or two important rules that
apply to everybody," he continued. "There can be no
hunting or *biting* or *eating* any other passenger.

No picking on neighbors who might be smaller or weaker. And no... *horsing* around, either."

He looked apologetically over at the various large quadrupeds of domestic type, and rather meaningfully at the cluster of monkeys who were having difficulty in sitting still.

"We all have to be quiet and patient until the end of the voyage. The rocking of the boat once we are under way might make it easier for you all to sleep quite a lot."

Atra-hasis gave a fine display of snoring. Several animals did the same in imitation and the parrots screeched.

"If you like, the boys can play their instruments for you: the girls can sing beautiful lullabies."

There was complete silence. Atra-hasis felt that the lions and elephants at least had taken his point. All the others sat without moving and appeared to be paying the greatest possible attention.

"I have worked everything out. The supplies of fodder and water will be enough for everyone if you are all considerate and fair."

He paused again, as if waiting for questions.

Instead there was a great breathing out, as if all the creatures in his care were relaxed and comfortable. Atra-hasis smiled.

Next he cut the first mark on one of the great, arching ribs of the coracle. So far, so good. One day successfully survived. It would be up to one of the boys to do the same every day. Upstairs there was a bowl of dates for the humans and some cool water but they were all too apprehensive to be hungry. As they sat together Atra-hasis suddenly raised his hand for complete silence. There was a tentative ping of raindrops thrumming on the roof. At first they were widely spaced, and then gradually, as they all strained to hear, they became more frequent, and much louder. The great boat quivered in response. They looked at one another in the half-darkness.

"It has begun," whispered Atra-hasis. "The Great Flood has begun."

All through that first day, when they felt the boat begin to move on the waters and the rain beat unrelentingly over their heads, Atra-hasis strode about peering at the walls or the lower deck, or looking up anxiously at the roof but no dampness or trickle was to be seen. Inside they could only try to envisage what was going on beyond the safety of their circular, bitumen-clad walls. In truth, the forces that had been unleashed were unimaginable.

The sources that were usually under the earth, the fountains, waterfalls and rivers joined with all the seas and a tempestuous blanket of the heaviest possible rain to cover the world with their waters. God Adad relinquished his most powerful storm winds to whirl all this into a destructive, heaving maelstrom that swept away, crushed and drowned all the work of man and all the work of nature. Where life had bustled about in all its richness and variety there was now only death and mud, at the bottom of such an earth-swallowing ocean as had never been seen before. And far above on the surface, buffeted by wind and rain, driven hither and yon by swirling currents and sudden gigantic waves, Atrahasis's round boat rose and fell, shuddered and spun around, but no drop of the driving waters got through the special coating, and every rescued form of life, enclosed in the warm and the dark, was safe.

It was increasingly stuffy with all the creatures together in the half-light, but nobody minded. There

was a strong feeling of purpose in the air, and it was infectious; somehow all of them seemed to have grasped that they were fortunate indeed to be inside their lifeboat. Sleep came easily with the ceaseless motion, and even when wide-awake none of the animals felt their normal round-the-clock urgency to find something to eat before dark (or in some cases, before light). Atra-hasis's supplies had been sensibly planned although there was always clearing up and cleaning up to be done on the lower deck. And then there were the bruises and bumps to be patched when four-legged animals, who really should have known better, got taken by surprise each time the great lifeboat lurched into a deep trough in the tumultuous waters outside.

For Atra-hasis's family it was good that there were constant tasks needing attention, and in fact they seemed to be on the go all the time. As a result they had no time to sit about and worry or think about what was happening; they had to move through the animal quarters peacefully, deal with whatever needed dealing with, and check that all were in good shape. Most of the large land mammals suffered terribly from seasickness for the first day or two.

The monkeys thought it very amusing to see the lions
and tigers, abandoning their stately demeanor,
groaning and miserable on the floor; one or two
of the most agile adopted a similar position,
imitating their pathetic moans with great
accuracy, but safely out of reach.

In the evenings Atra-hasis's family sat together
talking in low voices. They were all short of normal
sleep and often dozed off at the table. He looked
round at them. His older sons were growing beards,
and all the children looked older and more capable
by the day. The sight of them stilled the remaining
anxiety in his heart. The trusty boat piloted herself
through the waters and they would come through safe,
and when the time came they would all know what to
do. There was no sign of the youngest, now he looked,
but that was not surprising. Very-quick liked to climb
up inside the ribs and find a seat right under the roof,
whistling with the birds in their pairs and learning
their songs.

The gods, meanwhile, looked down tremulously,
some of them even covering their eyes. The reality
of the vast, dark ocean heaving languidly beneath
appalled them. Even the highest mountain tops
that had once formed familiar landmarks were now
invisible. No one could have suspected that, below
it all, the glittering, exuberant world that had been
their daily spectacle since time began had all been
destroyed forever.

What had they done?

The gods and goddesses were stricken and

dismayed and walked about like ghosts. Adad in particular was grim-faced but had absolutely nothing to say; they all knew he had merely been following orders. And Enlil himself, the dread architect of the awful plan, was suddenly nowhere to be found.

CHAPTER 8
The Boat Lands

No one aboard, human or otherwise, noticed at
first when the rain stopped, for they had all grown
accustomed to the thunderous drumming on the roof
as they lay about daydreaming or dozing. Eventually
someone pointed out that there was no more noise
from outside. Many of the animals woke up properly,
and there was a good deal of yawning and stretching
on all sides.

Their guardian found himself disconcerted,
shaking his head as if to unblock his ears, but soon it
struck Atra-hasis that if the rain really had stopped
then the water level outside would presumably start
to go down again. He stood sunk in thought, and
then he had an idea. They had taken the precaution
of setting a small but well-waterproofed hatch in the
roof on the off chance that it might be useful. He sent
Very-quick to climb up with a chisel to prise it open as
best he could.

"What can you see?"

"As far as I can see — which is not much from here," the boy called down, "there is just flat water in every direction. Nothing else."

"Where are my doves?"

They perched together on one of the wooden cross-braces, their usual immaculate selves despite the conditions all around them. He shaded his eyes as if searching the horizon and flapped his hands up and down. The male dove flew down onto his shoulder, and then up in a graceful curve to disappear through the hatch without touching its sides.

"How long do we have to wait, Hassy?"

"Until it gets dark, I should imagine."

It was fully dark and most of them had fallen back asleep by the time the solitary bird struggled bravely back through the half-open hatch. It came and landed on Atra-hasis's hand. He understood at once that the dove had found nowhere to perch in all those hours of flying, and he stroked the faithful bird in acknowledgment until it flew over to join its partner.

The same procedure was enacted the following day. The male dove wanted to go again himself but

everyone could
see that he was
still exhausted and
he sent the male
swallow instead.
Again it was a long
wait for everybody
and the fluttering wings were not heard again
until a similarly late hour.

Atra-hasis was worried by this stage, for what
would they do if the water just never went down?
It was with trepidation that he despatched one of
the ravens the next day, but this time, although they
waited patiently, the bird did not return, and he knew
then that the waters must now have receded to the
point that food and shelter were now available, at
least to those who could fly.

Soon after there came a dragged-out and
very alarming scraping sound. Atra-hasis winced,
expecting water to come rushing up through the
flooring, but his great boat slithered and tilted and
eventually it came to a stop. Then, with a dreadful
creaking and thumping the gigantic vessel began
to settle down. Everyone strained to hear.

At last, there was no more movement. They had landed.

The cavernous hold of the giant coracle rang out with cheers and roars and brays and squeaks and the human sons and daughters-in-law danced spontaneously round in a ring. Atra-hasis went for his axe. Surrounded by animals trying to see he carefully prized away the bitumen packing and knocked the door through. Fresh, cool air rushed in. Atra-hasis again held up his hand for quiet, and then he looked out.

They were perched on the side of a huge mountain. The boat had come to rest at a slight angle; it seemed to be firmly wedged and didn't feel too precarious, but they were definitely half way up a mountain. Fortunately the door was not far above the rocky surface.

"We do this carefully," said Atra-hasis. "I don't want any of you getting hurt. No mad jumping, however many legs you have. You all have a lot to do."

From his peculiar vantage point he could just make out through the mist that, far below, was land as well as water. And there was already greenery.

Their stock of animals, Atra-hasis was glad to see, disembarked with great politeness and "after you"-like gestures. They stood around in groups looking at the view, snuffing the air deeply and preparing themselves for the march ahead. As before, the large carried the small. The long line began to shuffle down the side of the mountain, stiffly at first, following a natural path in the rock, down, down to the clean and shining world beneath.

There was a sudden, familiar aroma in the air that made all the family left behind feel ravenous. Round a corner they found Atra-hasis praying to the gods in heaven, sacrificing and burning his spare livestock to show his intention from the first new moment to serve them as he had always done, and see to their needs.

The fragrant smoke wafted upwards in the clear air. The gods, who had not had a decent meal in weeks, noticed it immediately and flocked around appreciatively. Enki had been right, they agreed, and Enlil wrong. Without human beings there was no one to do the chores and look after them. What *had* they been thinking of? Well, they wouldn't be opting for mass destruction ever again, whatever happened.

There was an encouraging clink below, as
Atra-hasis put a couple of extra pieces on the coals.

Rather than any more upsets, they were thinking,
a few alterations could be made so that things could run
quietly and smoothly from now on.

"That captain fellow," said Enlil with his
mouth full, "What was his name again?"
"Atra-hasis," said Enki. "One of my best people."

"Yes, well, he has acted admirably... needs a *reward*...
everybody safe... the animals going back everywhere
already... Look for yourselves."

Many of the senior gods obediently peered down.
The animals had already reached the bottom of the
mountain and were starting to fan out in different
directions. The gods murmured agreement. Since so
many of them had thoroughly disapproved of the original
flood plan this new development was very cheering.

"What about eternal life?" suggested Enlil. "Seems
appropriate. I think he deserves it. We could see a bit
more of him. From time to time."

"I agree," said Enki, "Then he could be around
to supervise all the new developments."

"Indeed," said Enlil, yawning. "That's that then.
Tell me, is there any of that meat left?"

The human party, eventually, also set off down the path, carrying the bare minimum. Atra-hasis was sure that they would find everything they needed down below in due course. He turned for a last look at the huge boat, perched on the crags. She had done them proud. In his mind he saluted, with a lurch of the heart, all his poor perished craftsmen. And all of the others...

He sighed deeply. Their successors could now build anew, and again be strong. The two older boys ran on ahead with their young wives, hand in hand. There was a new, clean world right at their feet, and life to be created. And his youngest, likewise grown older and stronger day by day, strode by his father's side like a hero. They grinned at one another: the world would have its new future and life would proliferate everywhere. The gods were happy, the world would be reborn. His wife, walking close to them both, said nothing. She was certainly happy that their trials were over and confident about the trials to come, but it was annoying that she had already been bitten by one of their own mosquitoes.

Interlude

So, we have to imagine what happened to them afterwards. There are other cuneiform story tablets, some complete, some broken in pieces, but the struggles that lay ahead of Atra-hasis and his family are not recorded. The ancient Mesopotamian people knew, however, that life was indomitable, and that however angry their gods might be they would never allow complete annihilation of life. The plants and trees, animals and insects, birds and fish would all find safety and new life, and grow to bedeck the planet again and repopulate its waters.

One ancient document has survived to fill in one corner of the story. It is also a tablet of clay, maybe as much as 2,500 years old, that has both a written message in cuneiform and a drawn map of the world, the oldest map of the world ever discovered. Looking at this, examining its details, we can know a little more...

A Wanderer Comes

Many ages later, a Wanderer who was to become
famous himself left the Land of the Two Rivers
and traveled to the end of North and the end of
East. He went where none of his friends had been
before, far from the sunlight over the canals, up into
remote ranges of mountains where men, unafraid
of the snows, were few on the ground and spoke
unintelligible languages.

Beyond the mountains was a plain, endless it
seemed, his footsteps clear in the dust behind him
as he strode straight out into the unimaginable
distance. He walked thinking of nothing, his eyes
often closed in the thin, bright air. There was no
life and no sound, but for the scuff of his own
sandaled feet. After uncountable time the
Wanderer reached the very end of the world.

He stood still, breathing deeply, looking about
him. He had come to a river, vast and dark, shielding
its depths. He could not make out the far shore, but

he knew it must be a river and not a sea because the water swept before him, left to right. There was a small boat at the water's edge. He climbed in and pushed off. The boat pointed itself towards the invisible horizon and moved steadily forward, undeflected by the sideways-flowing current.

The boat sometimes rocked him to sleep and sometimes jerked him awake. He was neither hungry nor thirsty but when he trailed his fingers over the side he discovered that the water of the river was bitter.

Once he thought there might be a smudge on the horizon, straining to see, but decided it was only his imagination. Later he could definitely make out something dark and triangular, just above the hazy, dancing line. As his little craft plowed on he saw that what lay ahead of him was a vast mountain rising out of the water, huge and black, jagged even from afar like an upturned dagger. It grew steadily in front of his eyes as if it were alive, its profile stark and savage against the dark blue canopy of stars behind.

The boat reached the shoreline and gently came to a halt. He knew he must disembark, and climb. He was already at the first foothills, and soon he gained the mountain proper. It was bleak and lifeless, the rock itself shiny and difficult. A rough path swung away ahead of him, upwards and round towards a great craggy outcrop.

Suddenly the Wanderer stopped dead in his tracks, for far above him, silhouetted against the sky, he saw what he took to be a giant skeleton; the whitened, curved ribs of some monster camel that must have made its way up the mountain to die of starvation, stripped of its flesh by the sort of vultures that would come all the way to the end of the world.

But as he looked more closely he saw that the ribs could not be those of an animal, for they were of wood, not bone, and each the same shape and size. And, as he gazed transfixed in the loneliness of the dark mountain, the words of the old story came back into the Wanderer's mind. How the hero Atra-hasis, proud of his construction, had described the ribs of his life-saving boat as "thick as a barley barrel," just as these ancient wooden ribs above his head, huge and squat, were as thick as a barley barrel. So it came to the Wanderer as he stood alone at the edge of the world, that here was the wreck of Atra-hasis's life-saving boat from the time before the flood.

Inside that rib cage, once upon a time, had waited all the animals, safe and dry. And this was the famous mountain where Atra-hasis's great, round craft had landed when the waters went down. And it had been there ever since, seen by nobody, visited by no one.

He must return as fast as he could, he decided, as he clambered back down the slippery path, relieved to find the waiting boat, eager to retrace his solitary path far across the empty plain and the snow-tipped mountains. Now he could explain to everyone where Mount Nitsir, with the remains of the Ark, was really to be found.

Perhaps they wouldn't believe him. He would have to write it down, draw a picture. Yes, thought the Wanderer, when he got home he could make a map.

"To the Fourth Mountain, you must travel seven Leagues..."

He nodded to himself. If they took the trouble, there it would be, waiting.

"... barley-barrel thick are its wood blocks; ten fingers thick its..."

That would show them...

Following Atra-hasis's Instructions

The instructions that are such an important part of the ancient Babylonian story are so precise and careful that anyone reading a translation of the words might think that, with their help, Atra-hasis's boat could be built today. And that is exactly what has happened. A team of experts and skilful boat-building workmen built a replica of the great round boat as an experiment, by the side of a lake in Kerala in India. It was constructed using the materials listed in the tablet, not full size, but exactly to scale, and the result was certainly the biggest coracle that the world has ever seen. It took four months to build, and it floated beautifully when we launched it, watched by a television crew who recorded every step for a documentary film. It was like making a giant wedding cake using a 4,000-year-old recipe. What a great adventure!